TUBA

CHRISTMAS FAVORITES

Solos and Band Arrangements
Correlated with Essential Elements Band Method

ARRANGED BY
MICHAEL SWEENEY

Welcome to Essential Elements Christmas Favorites! There are two versions of each holiday selection in this versatile book:
1. The SOLO version (with lyrics) appears on the left-hand page.
2. The FULL BAND arrangement appears on the right-hand page.
Use the optional accompaniment tape when playing solos for friends and family. Your director may also use the accompaniment tape in band rehearsals and concerts.

ISBN 978-0-7935-1765-7

HAL•LEONARD®
CORPORATION
7777 W. BLUEMOUND RD. P.O. BOX 13819 MILWAUKEE, WI 53213

JINGLE BELLS

Words and Music by J. PIERPONT
Arranged by MICHAEL SWEENEY

Solo

JINGLE BELLS

Words and Music by J. PIERPONT
Arranged by MICHAEL SWEENEY

Band Arrangement

00862514

UP ON THE HOUSETOP

Arranged by MICHAEL SWEENEY

Solo

UP ON THE HOUSETOP

Band Arrangement

Arranged by MICHAEL SWEENEY

00862514

THE HANUKKAH SONG

Arranged by MICHAEL SWEENEY

Solo

THE HANUKKAH SONG

Band Arrangement

Arranged by MICHAEL SWEENEY

00862514

A HOLLY JOLLY CHRISTMAS

Music and Lyrics by JOHNNY MARKS
Arranged by MICHAEL SWEENEY

Solo

A Holly Jolly Christmas

Band Arrangement

Music and Lyrics by **JOHNNY MARKS**
Arranged by MICHAEL SWEENEY

WE WISH YOU A MERRY CHRISTMAS

Solo

Arranged by MICHAEL SWEENEY

WE WISH YOU A MERRY CHRISTMAS

Band Arrangement

Arranged by MICHAEL SWEENEY

00862514

FROSTY THE SNOW MAN

Words and Music by STEVE NELSON and JACK ROLLINS
Arranged by MICHAEL SWEENEY

Solo

FROSTY THE SNOW MAN

Words and Music by STEVE NELSON and JACK ROLLINS
Arranged by MICHAEL SWEENEY

Band Arrangement

00862514

ROCKIN' AROUND THE CHRISTMAS TREE

Music and Lyrics by JOHNNY MARKS
Arranged by MICHAEL SWEENEY

Solo

ROCKIN' AROUND THE CHRISTMAS TREE

Music and Lyrics by JOHNNY MARKS
Arranged by MICHAEL SWEENEY

Band Arrangement

JINGLE-BELL ROCK

Words and Music by JOE BEAL and JIM BOOTHE
Arranged by MICHAEL SWEENEY

Solo

JINGLE-BELL ROCK

Words and Music by JOE BEAL
and JIM BOOTHE
Arranged by MICHAEL SWEENEY

Band Arrangement

00862514

RUDOLPH THE RED-NOSED REINDEER

Music and Lyrics by JOHNNY MARKS
Arranged by MICHAEL SWEENEY

Solo

RUDOLPH THE RED-NOSED REINDEER

Music and Lyrics by JOHNNY MARKS
Arranged by MICHAEL SWEENEY

Band Arrangement

LET IT SNOW!
LET IT SNOW! LET IT SNOW!

Words by SAMMY CAHN
Music by JULE STYNE
Arranged by MICHAEL SWEENEY

Solo

LET IT SNOW! LET IT SNOW! LET IT SNOW!

Band Arrangement

Words by SAMMY CAHN
Music by JULE STYNE
Arranged by MICHAEL SWEENEY

00862514

THE CHRISTMAS SONG

Music and Lyric by MEL TORME and ROBERT WELLS
Arranged by MICHAEL SWEENEY

Solo

THE CHRISTMAS SONG

Music and Lyric by MEL TORME and ROBERT WELLS

Arranged by MICHAEL SWEENEY

Band Arrangement